PLACES IN MY COMMUNITY

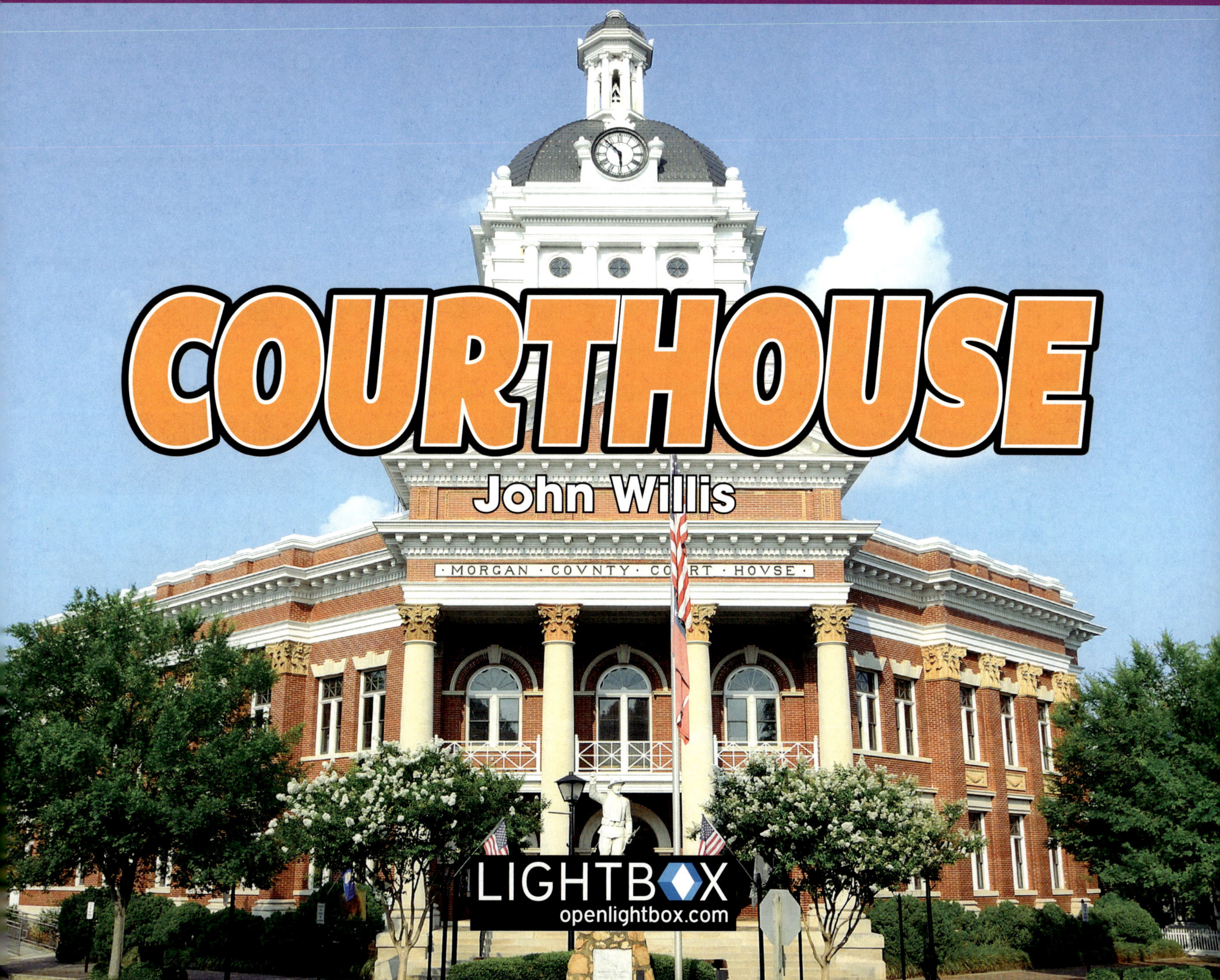

COURTHOUSE

John Willis

LIGHTBOX
openlightbox.com

Lightbox is an all-inclusive digital solution for the teaching and learning of curriculum topics in an original, groundbreaking way. Lightbox is based on National Curriculum Standards.

OPTIMIZED FOR

- ✓ **TABLETS**
- ✓ **WHITEBOARDS**
- ✓ **COMPUTERS**
- ✓ **AND MUCH MORE!**

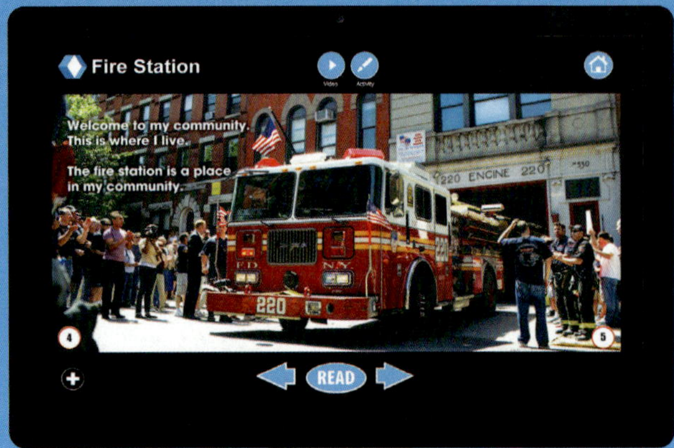

STANDARD FEATURES OF LIGHTBOX

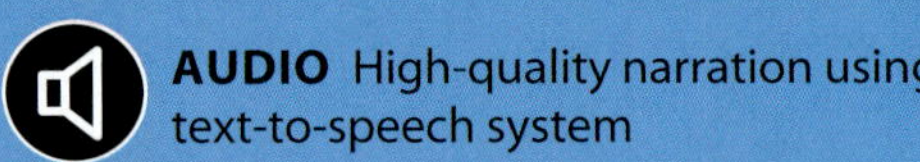
AUDIO High-quality narration using text-to-speech system

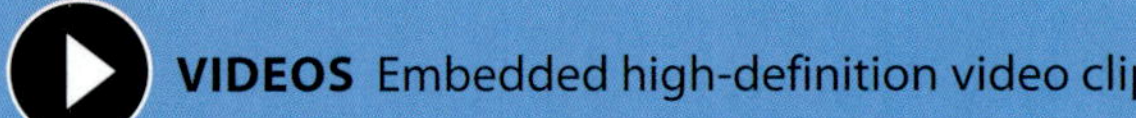
VIDEOS Embedded high-definition video clips

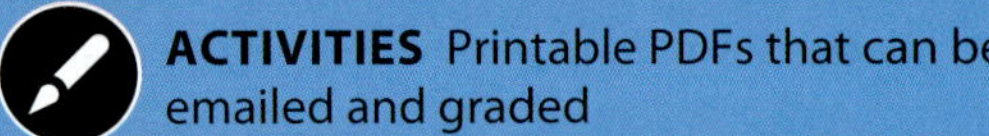
ACTIVITIES Printable PDFs that can be emailed and graded

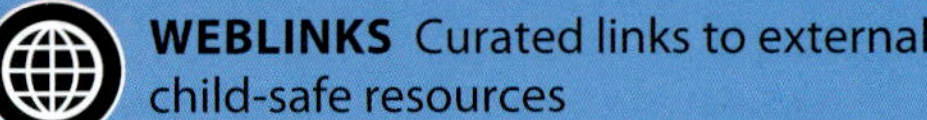
WEBLINKS Curated links to external, child-safe resources

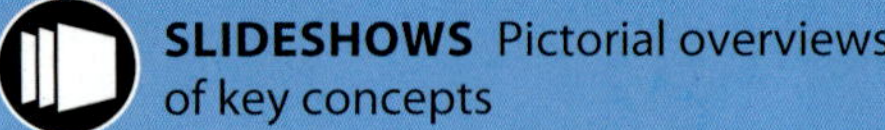
SLIDESHOWS Pictorial overviews of key concepts

INTERACTIVE MAPS Interactive maps and aerial satellite imagery

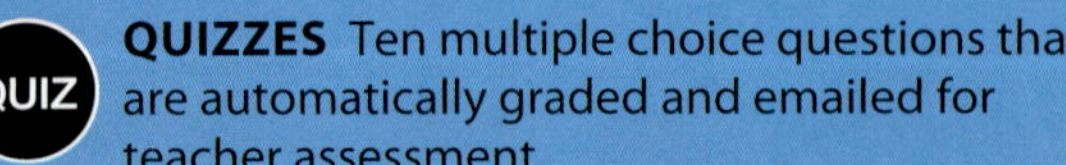
QUIZZES Ten multiple choice questions that are automatically graded and emailed for teacher assessment

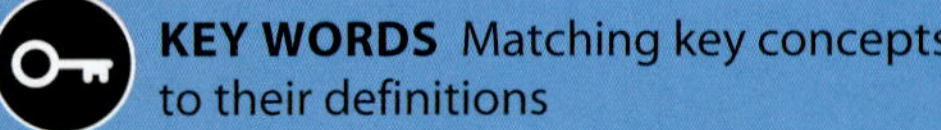
KEY WORDS Matching key concepts to their definitions

VIDEOS

WEBLINKS

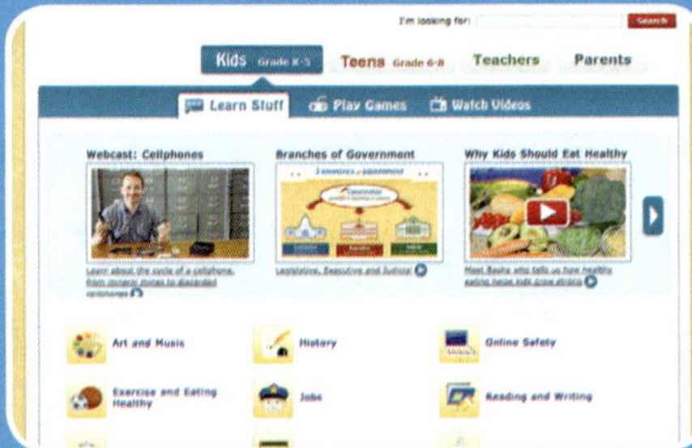

SLIDESHOWS

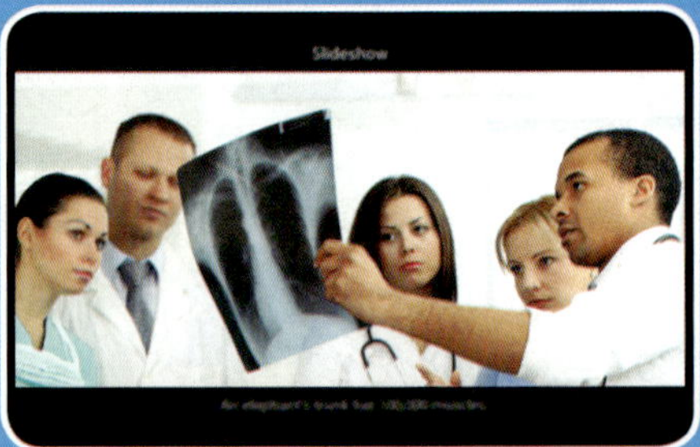

QUIZZES

COURTHOUSE

In this book, you will learn about

courthouses

the people who work there

why they are important

and much more!

Welcome to my community.
This is where I live.

The courthouse is a place in my community.

The courthouse is a place people may go to settle a problem.

A judge listens to each person's story and helps decide who is right.

The **King William Courthouse** in Virginia is one of the oldest courthouses in the United States.

Each courthouse has one or more courtrooms. Most people in a courtroom sit behind a short wall called the bar.

Lawyers and judges work on the other side of the bar. This part of the courtroom is called the well.

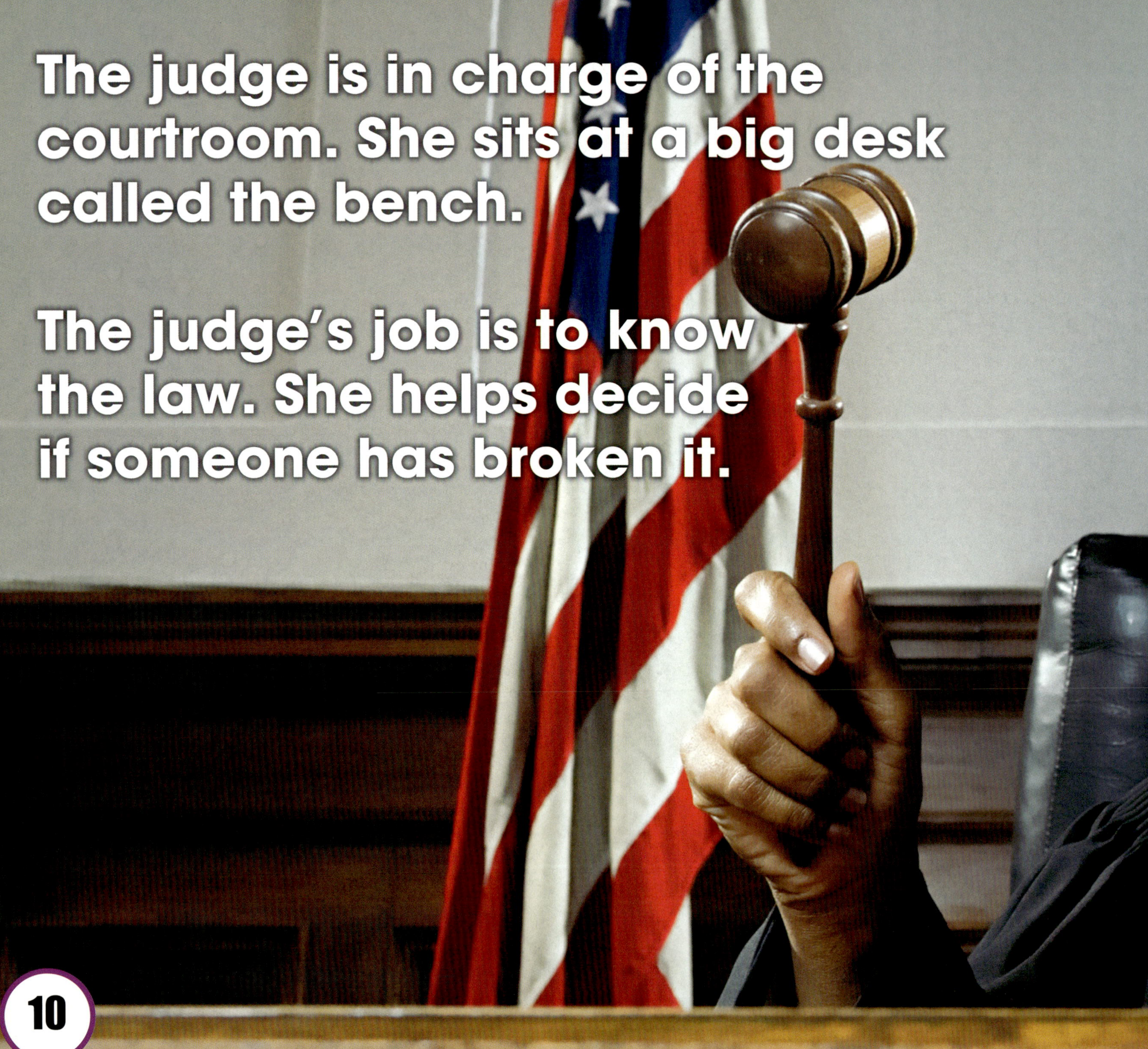

The judge is in charge of the courtroom. She sits at a big desk called the bench.

The judge's job is to know the law. She helps decide if someone has broken it.

Lawyers understand the law. People pay lawyers to speak for them in court.

A lawyer may help a person who has been hurt in an accident.

Harvard Law School has trained lawyers for more than **200** years.

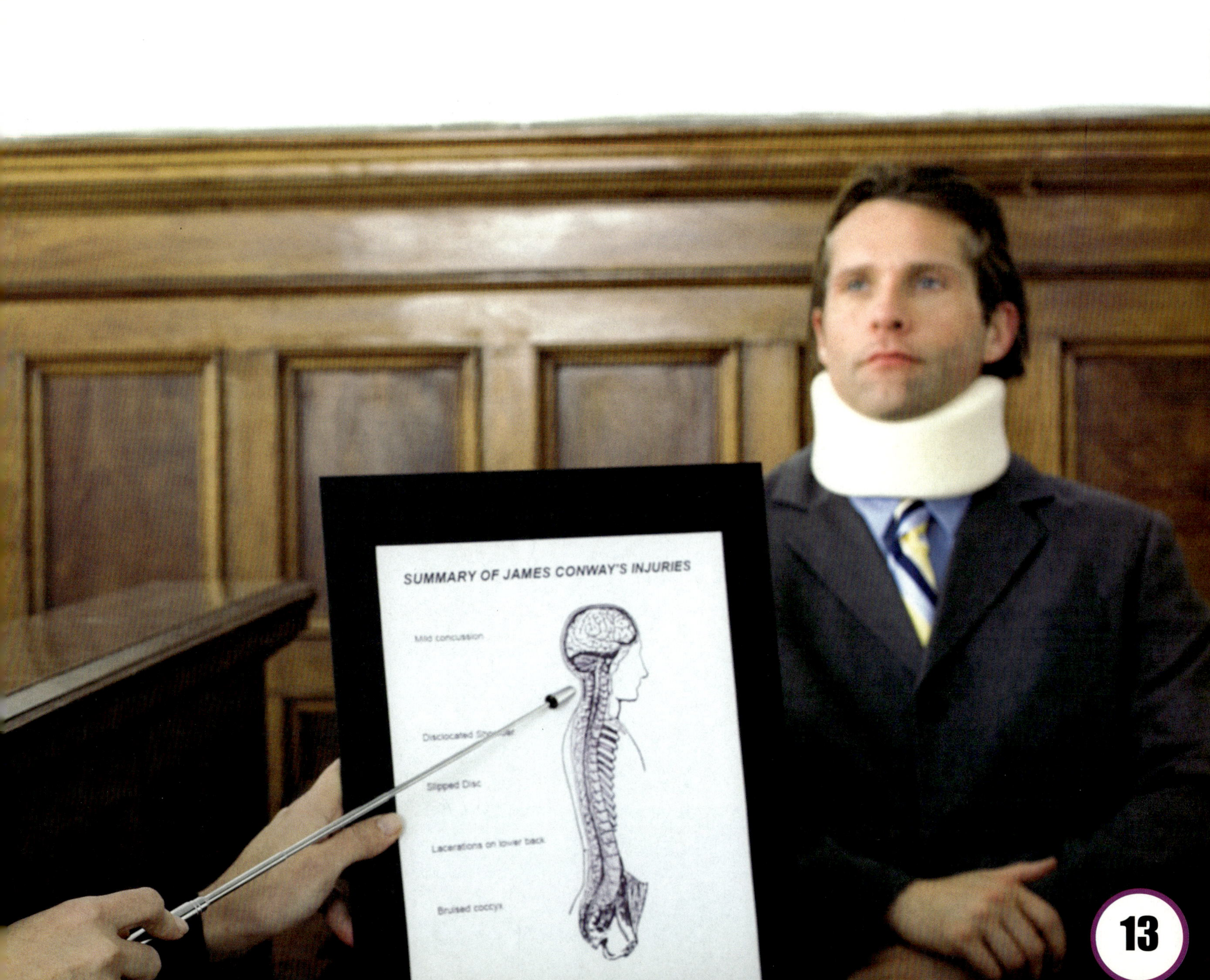
SUMMARY OF JAMES CONWAY'S INJURIES
Mild concussion
Dislocated
Slipped Disc
Lacerations on lower back
Bruised coccyx

Court reporters keep track of everything that happens in court.

They use special machines to write what people say and do.

Court reporters must be able **to type** more than **225 words** a minute.

People in my community may be asked to be part of a jury.

A jury is a group of people that helps decide if a person did something wrong.

A jury is made of **6** to **12** people.

My class will take a field trip to the courthouse. We might get to be part of a pretend jury.

Some lawyers work for free.

They work for people in my community that can not pay for help in court.

See what you have learned about courthouses and the people who work there.

Which of these pictures does not show a courthouse?

KEY WORDS

Research has shown that as much as 65 percent of all written material published in English is made up of 300 words. These 300 words cannot be taught using pictures or learned by sounding them out. They must be recognized by sight. This book contains 68 common sight words to help young readers improve their reading fluency and comprehension. This book also teaches young readers several important content words, such as proper nouns. These words are paired with pictures to aid in learning and improve understanding.

Page	Sight Words First Appearance
4	I, is, live, my, this, to, where
5	a, in, place, the
7	and, each, go, helps, may, of, one, people, right, states, story, who
8	has, more, most, or
9	on, other, part, side, well, work
10	at, big, if, it, know, she
12	an, been, for, than, them, years
15	be, do, keep, must, say, that, they, use, what, words, write
16	did, group, made, something
18	get, might, take, we, will
20	can, not, some

Page	Content Words First Appearance
4	community
5	courthouse
7	judge, King William Courthouse, person, problem
8	bar, courtrooms, lawyers, wall, well
10	bench, desk, job, law
12	accident, court, Harvard Law School
15	court reporters, machines, minute
16	jury
18	class, field trip

Published by Smartbook Media Inc.
350 5th Avenue, 59th Floor New York, NY 10118
Website: www.openlightbox.com

Library of Congress Cataloging-in-Publication Data

Names: Willis, John, 1989- author.
Title: Courthouse / John Willis.
Description: New York, NY : Smartbook Media Inc., [2016] | Series: Places in my community | Includes index.
Identifiers: LCCN 2016051535 (print) | LCCN 2016059077 (ebook) | ISBN 9781510518834 (hard cover : alk. paper) | ISBN 9781510518841 (multi-user ebk.)
Subjects: LCSH: Justice, Administration of--United States--Juvenile literature. | Courthouses--United States--Juvenile literature.
Classification: LCC KF8700 .W49 2016 (print) | LCC KF8700 (ebook) | DDC 347.73/1--dc23
LC record available at https://lccn.loc.gov/2016051535

Printed in the United States of America in Brainerd, Minnesota
1 2 3 4 5 6 7 8 9 0 20 19 18 17 16

122016
111816

Project Coordinator: Jared Siemens
Designer: Ana María Vidal

Every reasonable effort has been made to trace ownership and to obtain permission to reprint copyright material. The publisher would be pleased to have any errors or omissions brought to its attention so that they may be corrected in subsequent printings.

The publisher acknowledges Alamy, Dreamstime, Shutterstock, Getty Images, and iStock as its primary image suppliers for this title.